PIANO • VOCAL • GUITAR

THE BEST OF WORSHIP TOGETHER ®

ISBN 0-634-08278-7

7777 W. BLUEMOUND RD. P.O. BOX 13819 MILWAUKEE, WI 53213

Visit Hal Leonard Online at
www.halleonard.com

CONTENTS

BETTER IS ONE DAY

Words and Music by
MATT REDMAN

Moderately, with a strong beat

How love-ly is Your dwell-ing place,
thing I ask and I would seek:

O Lord Al-might - y,   for my soul longs and
to see Your beau - ty,   to find You in the

e - ven faints for You,   for
place Your glo - ry dwells.   One

FOREVER

Words and Music by
CHRIS TOMLIN

GIVE US CLEAN HANDS

Words and Music by
CHARLIE HALL

We bow our ___ hearts, we bend our ___ knees.

Oh Spir - it, come make us hum - ble. We turn our ___ eyes

from e - vil ___ things. Oh Lord, we cast out our i -

18

THE HAPPY SONG

Words and Music by
MARTIN SMITH

Oh,   I   could   sing   un — end — ing
I   could   dance   a   thou — sand

end - ing songs of how You saved my soul. _

Well, I could dance a

thou - sand miles be - cause of Your great love. _

Ev - 'ry - bod - y,

GOD OF WONDERS

Words and Music by MARC BYRD
and STEVE HINDALONG

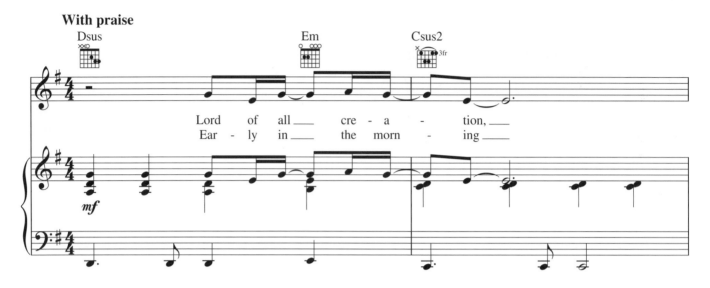

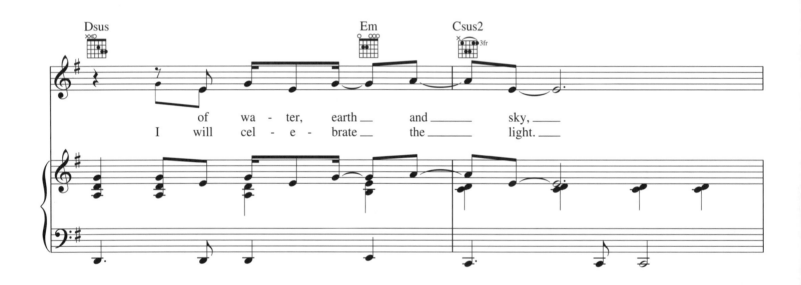

HE REIGNS

Words and Music by PETER FURLER
and STEVE TAYLOR

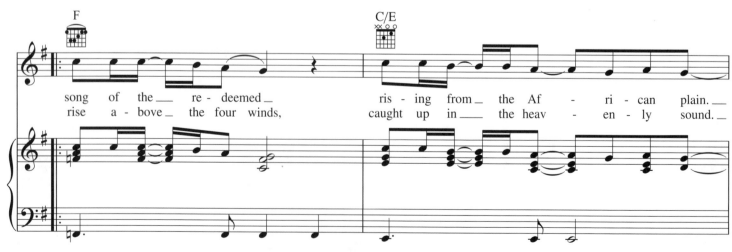

It's the

song of the __ re- deemed __ ris- ing from the Af- ri- can plain.
rise a- bove __ the four winds, caught up in __ the heav- en- ly sound. __

THE HEART OF WORSHIP

Words and Music by
MATT REDMAN

HERE I AM TO WORSHIP

Words and Music by
TIM HUGHES

- er know____ how much____ it cost____ to see____ my sin____ up - on____

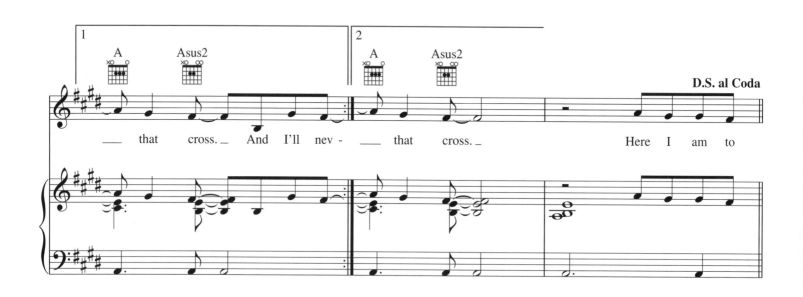

D.S. al Coda

____ that cross.____ And I'll nev-____ that cross.____ Here I am to

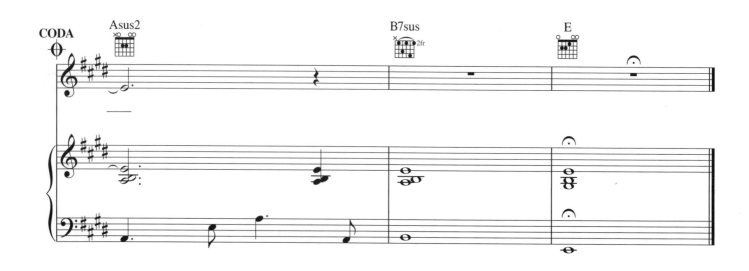

CODA

I COULD SING OF YOUR LOVE FOREVER

Words and Music by
MARTIN SMITH

JESUS, LOVER OF MY SOUL

Words and Music by
PAUL OAKLEY

LET EVERYTHING THAT HAS BREATH

Words and Music by
MATT REDMAN

KINDNESS

Words and Music by LOUIE GIGLIO,
JESSE REEVES and CHRIS TOMLIN

(1., 2.) O - pen up _____ the skies _____ of mer - cy
(3.) We can feel _____ Your mer - cy fall - ing.

and rain down _____ the cleans - ing _____ flood. _____
You are turn - ing our hearts back _____ a - gain.

ONCE AGAIN

Words and Music by
MATT REDMAN

68

WE WANT TO SEE JESUS LIFTED HIGH

Words and Music by
DOUG HORLEY

72

74

-sus lift - ed high. ___ We want to see, we want to see,

(clap)

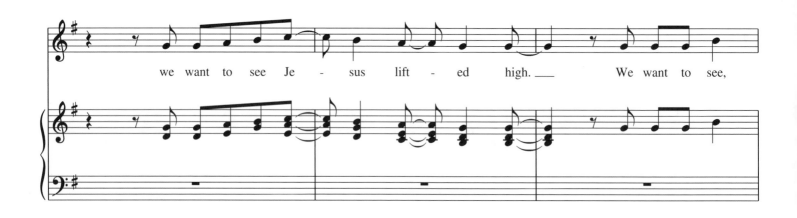

we want to see Je - sus lift - ed high. ___ We want to see,

we want to see, we want to see Je - sus lift - ed high. __

(clap) *(clap)*

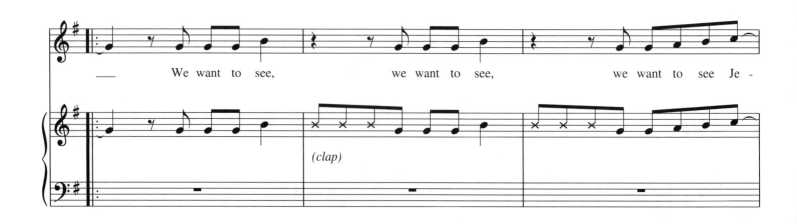

___ We want to see, we want to see, we want to see Je -

(clap)

YOU ALONE

Words and Music by JACK PARKER
and DAVID CROWDER

More Contemporary Christian Folios from Hal Leonard

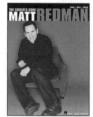